HEALED
—— FROM THE ——
WOUNDS
—— OF MY ——
PAST!

ADDIE KENNEBREW

HEALED FROM THE WOUNDS OF MY PAST!
Published by Purposely Created Publishing Group™
Copyright © 2020 Addie Kennebrew

All rights reserved.

No part of this book may be reproduced, distributed or transmitted in any form by any means, graphic, electronic, or mechanical, including photocopy, recording, taping, or by any information storage or retrieval system, without permission in writing from the publisher, except in the case of reprints in the context of reviews, quotes, or references.

Printed in the United States of America

ISBN: 978-1-64484-266-9

Special discounts are available on bulk quantity purchases by book clubs, associations and special interest groups. For details email: sales@publishyourgift.com or call (888) 949-6228. For information log on to www.PublishYourGift.com

HEALED
—— FROM THE ——
WOUNDS
—— OF MY ——
PAST!

First and foremost, I would like to give praise and honor to my Lord and Savior, Jesus Christ! I thank Him for saving my soul on January 3, 1995. I thank Him for giving me the courage and the strength to write this book. This is something that I have felt led to do for a very long time. I would like to give honor to my wonderful husband for always encouraging me and being my greatest supporter. I would like to thank God for my children who have always motivated me and supported me in all of my endeavors.

Table of Contents

Preface ix
Chapter 1: The Journey and Healing Begin...... 1
Chapter 2: Wounded and Weary..................... 11
Chapter 3: Forgive So You Can Be Healed 19
Chapter 4: You Don't Have to Be a
Product of Your Environment........................ 23
Chapter 5: The Journey Was Not Easy 31
Chapter 6: Don't Let Life Make You Bitter
but Better 39
Chapter 7: Free Indeed 45
Chapter 8: Your Past Doesn't Define You 57
Chapter 9: Deliverance Is Coming to
Your House 63
Chapter 10: A Change Is Going to Come 71
Chapter 11: Speak the Word.......................... 79
Chapter 12: One Touch 87
Chapter 13: He Is a Miracle Worker.............. 97
Chapter 14: He that Is Without Sin Cast
the First Stone 103
Daily Confessions... 115
Daily Affirmations.. 117
Sources... 121
About the Author 123

Preface

I will never forget my trial sermon in 1999. It was called "I Am Healed from the Wounds of My Past." That message was so full of passion, love, and power. I can remember the service as I am writing this book. People, along with myself, were in awe at the grace and power of God that was manifested on that particular day. I remember preaching from 2 Corinthians 5:17, "Therefore, if anyone is in Christ, he is a new creation; old things have passed away; behold, all things have become new. Psalm 103:12 says, "As far as the east is from the west, so far has he removed our transgression from us." It doesn't matter what man remembers; you have been forgiven if you have accepted Jesus Christ as your Lord and Savior.

Things that I used to do I don't do anymore. Places I used to go I don't go anymore. I have a new way of walking, talking, and living.

"For I know the plans I have for you," declares the LORD, "plans to prosper you and not to harm you, plans to give you hope and a future."

—JEREMIAH 29:11, NIV

CHAPTER 1
The Journey and Healing Begin

There was a woman in Luke 13:11-12 who had a spirit of infirmity for eighteen years. The Merriam-Webster.com dictionary defines infirmity as "the quality or state of being infirm, the condition of being feeble: frailty." This woman's illness was caused by a spirit. In other words, a spirit was behind her problem. Jesus was able to identify the spirit, and that's what I love so much about this story. In the New Living Translation of the Bible, it says that she was bent double and could not straighten up at all. It does not say that she did not want to straighten up. The spirit that had her bound would not let her straighten up. There are a lot of people who have had double trouble to hit their lives that got them all bent out of shape, and it doesn't matter how hard they have tried to straighten up; they have not been able to do so. Some have tried to straighten up their lives for many years, but they have not been able to because they have not been able to identify the root cause of their problem. I believe that in order for a person to be delivered from a spirit, it has to be identified. Jesus saw what others could not see concerning this woman's infirmity. The things that have kept you bound and down in your spirit have to loose you and let you go. The Bible goes on to tell us when Jesus saw her, He called her over and said to her, "Woman, thou are loosed from your infirmity." I decree in the name of Jesus Christ of Nazareth that Jesus sees your infirmity, your pain, and your suffering. I hear, "Man and woman, you are loosed from your pain, your addiction, your suffering, and your infirmity!" In the midst of this woman's infirmity, she still went to the synagogue. Too many times, we allow infirmities, weakness, pain, suffering, insecurities, sin, shame, and diseases to keep us out of church. It is very important that we be at the right place at the right time. This woman could have missed her divine healing if she would've had a pity party and said, "I have been tithing, ushering, serving, and faithful my entire life, and I have not received my healing." Her healing was tied to her faithfulness.

She went to church in spite of her condition. We cannot afford to let what we are going through stop us from attending church. We must press our way in the midst of the storm.

    I will never forget attending a tent revival in 1995. I was tired of living the lifestyle that I was living. I was ready for a change. My mind was made up, and no one was going to change my mind. I knew I wanted to give my life to God. I was so excited to attend that meeting that night because I felt in my spirit something great was going to happen. As I reflect on that night, I can see the hand of God leading me and guiding me. Think about it, if I had stayed home on that particular night, I probably would not be saved today or a preacher. I was tired of living a lifestyle of sin. There is truly a blessing in your pressing. I was determined that nothing or nobody was going to stop me that night. There have been many times when I didn't feel like going to church or to a revival, but when I put aside my feelings and followed the leading of the Holy Spirit, there was a blessing with my name on it. It is funny how the enemy tries to fight you on Saturday night and Sunday morning. He doesn't want you to receive that word, your healing, your miracle, or your breakthrough. If this woman had stayed at home on that particular day, she would have missed her moment. Do you know who was behind her attack? Satan was, but Jesus was about to counteract the devil's attack! I wonder who is behind your attack? I have news for you; I don't care who is behind your attack. You are about to be delivered and set free! It doesn't matter how many years it has been. This is your season to be set free. Let's look at Luke 13:16. "And ought not this woman, being a daughter of Abraham, whom Satan has bound be set free on the Sabbath day from what bound her?" Satan was behind her problem, but Jesus was the solution to her problem. The enemy wants to cripple your life. Cripple is defined in the Merriam-Webster.com dictionary as being "lame, flawed, or imperfect." This woman could not lift her head up because the spirit of infirmity had her double bent. There are people who are reading this book who have not been able to lift their heads up because of shame, rape, slander, foreclosure, bankruptcy, divorce, business failure, diseases, and false accusations. The enemy has kept you bound long enough! Not only are you going to be able to lift up your head, but God is also about to lift up your spirit. God is about to lift up your family. "Lift up your heads, O you gates! And be lifted up, you everlasting doors! And the King of glory shall come in. Who is this King of glory? The LORD strong and mighty, the LORD mighty in battle" (Psalm 24:7-10, KJV). Your days of walking around with your head down are over. This is your season to be set free! I decree and declare that you are healed from the wounds of your past. Satan can no longer keep you down or in darkness or in bondage. "The spirit of the Lord is upon me, because he has anointed me to preach the gospel to the poor. He has sent me to proclaim release to the captives, And recovery of the sight to the blind. To set free those who are oppressed, to proclaim the favorable year of the Lord" (Luke 4:18, NASB). When you are in your darkest season, just know that the sun is going to shine again. There is a light at the end of the tunnel. I'm reminded of the word in the Bible that says we can cast all of our anxiety on him because he cares for us (1 Peter 5:7, NIV). If no one else cares, Jesus cares for you. Not only does Jesus care for us, but He is also concerned about what we are going through in life. "For God so loved the world, that he gave his only begotten Son, that whosoever believeth in him should not perish, but have everlasting life" (John 3:16, KJV). Jesus was anointed to destroy every yoke and remove every burden. We must acknowledge that God's spirit and anointing is not on everyone. Jesus knew that He was anointed for the assignment that God had entrusted to him. I believe that when you are anointed and appointed by God, you are unstoppable. It is the anointing that destroys the yoke. There are people who are in my ministry who have been delivered from drugs, alcoholism, and demonic oppression because of the anointing. They came in yoked up but left free.

"But he was wounded for our transgressions, he was bruised for our iniquities: the chastisement of our peace was upon him; and with his stripes we are healed."

—ISAIAH 53:5, KJV

Chapter 2

Wounded and Weary

My process of being healed from the wounds of the past started early in my Christian walk. Walk it out! There were some things in my life that only I could walk out.

I was wounded and weary, and I didn't even know it. I would sometimes find myself going into the bathroom, weeping and talking to God about what was on my heart. I was a wounded child, teenager, and adult. In spite of what I felt on the inside, I still loved God. God was the one who took a wounded and weary soul and made her whole again. I eventually learned that God would become everything that I needed in life. After losing my mom as a teenager, I had to take on the role of an adult to help raise my sister. Even though we lost our mother at an early age, God was still with us. He said in His word that He will never leave you nor forsake you. (Deuteronomy 31:6, KJV). In my darkest hour, God was still there. As I grew up, I came into the knowledge of the truth that weeping may endure for a night, but joy cometh in the morning (Psalm 30:5, KJV). When I look back over my life, I can see that all of the weeping, pain, suffering, and night seasons I experienced at such a young and tender age were birthing pains to prepare me for my ministry.

I had my good days and my bad days. There were days I would be fine, and my mind never wandered off into wonderland. What I mean by "wonderland" is wondering what my life would have been like if I was not brought up in the negative environment where there was violence, alcoholism, abuse, homicide, and no guidance. I thank God for my mom and stepdad because they did the best they could, raising and providing for their children. God had a greater plan and purpose for my life. I had flashbacks concerning my childhood. I saw myself walking up and down the streets, playing in the rain and the sunshine. I saw all of my cousins and me playing with cardboard boxes, sliding off the hill, and playing ball with milk jugs and sticks. I saw my cousins and me walking and talking, looking up in the sky talking about Jesus and exploring in the woods. As children, we picked plums, apples, pears, berries, and muscadines. We went swimming almost everyday in the creek and city pool during the summer. We had birthday parties along the creek side. It was as if the Lord had given us our own beach in the hood. Believe it or not, it actually had sand and snakes too. The snakes used to be on the branches while we were swimming. I guess when they got tired of watching us swim, they slithered in the water. Now, there is no way on God's green earth I would swim in a pool or creek if I saw a snake on the branches or in the water. One thing I know for sure is that God did not allow a snake to bite any of us. As my mom would say, "The good Lord was looking out for us." My mind went back to my cousins and me swimming in the same creek that we called Carrville Wash Hole. I remember one day my cousin was being sucked up in a sinkhole, and I was in her reach. She grabbed me, and we were both sucked in. My cousin's sibling saved us both that day. We both were good swimmers; however, there was a force in the water that we could not control. When there is a great calling on your life, the enemy will try to take you out prematurely. When you grow up and pay more attention to situations and circumstances in life, you will see that most children who had a rough childhood or who went through a lot as a child are the ones who God raised up to impact the world. Most of them came from broken homes or faced some type of trauma in life. God had his hands on us, and we did not know it. Isaiah 43:2 confirms it. "When you pass through the water, I will be with you; and when you pass through the rivers, they will not sweep over you."

I had no idea that the things I had to go through as a child and as a young adult were preparing me for ministry. God used all of the pain, the suffering, and the abuse to prepare me for my destiny. I came to the realization that your pain will have a purpose. I am a firm believer that what you go through is not just for you but for someone else. No pain, no gain. No test, no testimony. No cross, no crown. I believe that we all have a cross to bear. Some may not be as painful as others. My cross may not be your cross, and your cross may not be my cross, but God's grace is sufficient. Luke 9:23 in the King James Version says, "Then he said unto his disciples, 'If any man will come after Me, let him deny himself take up his cross and follow after me.'" During this time, I understood very little about this verse. All I know is I was going through some hardships and difficulties at a very young age.

I remember being cut in my face when I was a teenager. It resulted in getting twenty-five stitches. I do not believe it was intentional. I have no ill feelings toward my family member. As a matter of fact, I love him dearly. As the years passed, I eventually became his pastor, and I had the privilege and the honor of leading him to Christ. God also allowed me to help him get his driver's license back. He actually drove my truck, and we both were extremely happy that he passed his road test. There are good people in this world who have made some wrong choices in life. I have, and many of you who are reading this book have also. It doesn't mean that you are a bad person. Good people sometimes make bad decisions and wrong choices in life. I remember breaking a bottle and cutting another teenager. I must tell the truth and shame the devil. It's hard to believe, but I did. I went from breaking bottles to breaking chains and breaking generational curses. Won't He do it! I modeled what I saw.

"Holding a grudge doesn't make you strong;
it makes you bitter.
Forgiving doesn't make you weak;
it sets you free."

−DAVIS WILLIS

Chapter 3

Forgive So You Can Be Healed

I've learned that you can do a thousand things right and one thing wrong, and people will always remember the one thing you did wrong. I am so glad that God is not like man. Isaiah 43:25 says, "I am He who blots out your transgression for my own sake, and I will not remember your sins." It doesn't matter what you have done or how many mistakes you have made. God is not like man. He is not going to bring up what you use to do. His love for us is not conditional. When you repent for your sins, you are forgiven. There are many who will try to bring up your past mistakes to try to degrade you. The next time the enemy brings up your past be sure to tell him that Jesus dropped the charges. "For all have sinned and come short of the glory of God;" (Romans 3:23, KJV). If we cannot forgive men of their trespasses towards us, then God cannot forgive us. When you truly forgive someone, you don't keep bringing up what they did to you. I am sharing my story as a testimony to the power of forgiveness and redemption. We must forgive, so we can be healed. Forgiveness is for you. Forgiveness doesn't mean that you have to return to a relationship. Forgiving doesn't mean forgetting nor does it mean that you've given the message that what someone did was okay. It just means that you've let go of the anger or guilt towards someone or towards yourself. That can be easier said than done. Jesus said, "Father, forgive them, for they do not know what they are doing" (Luke 23:34, NIV). Stephanie A. Sarkis states, "If forgiveness was easy, everyone would do it." The word says, "But if you do not forgive men their trespasses, neither will your father forgive your trespasses" (Matthew 6:15, NKJV). It is time to take your power back. You owe it to yourself. You cannot change what happened to you, but you can control how long you hold onto the pain, the resentment, and the un-forgiveness. I did not grow up with a blame game mentality nor did I grow up thinking that the world owed me something because of my upbringing.

"I didn't grow up having role models. I grew up having people I didn't want to be like and seeing situations I'd never want to be in. Not all of us are dealt the right cards, but that doesn't mean you can't reshuffle your deck for a better outcome."

—UNKNOWN

Chapter 4
You Don't Have to Be a Product of Your Environment

I remember going with my mom to pick peas, pecans, and other items, trying to make enough money to buy household supplies and whatever else she was going to spend the money on. I understood at an early age that it was still mom's money. My mom was a clean freak. She was going to make sure she had household supplies to keep her house clean. I don't know anyone who could wash clothes in a foot tub and by hand as good as my mom. Eventually, we moved on up and got a new washing machine. I learned at an early age about working for what you want.

My mom also cleaned homes and a local church in our city. I remember cleaning the church with my mom on several occasions. I think it is hilarious how I went from cleaning a church to pastoring a church, cleaning souls through the preaching of God's holy word. I was taught responsibility at an early age. I had no choice but to grow up fast and learn the street life. Everyone considered grown is not mature. As a child and a teenager, I enjoyed hanging around older people because I understood their language. Some said I had an old soul. I always had a mind of my own, and I was going to speak what was on my mind. I recall going to different family members and neighbors' homes, sitting around listening to them talk about life and what was going on in the neighborhood. I was never told to stay away from such and such house because everyone knew you, and everyone was like family in our neighborhood. The majority of all the cousins and friends in the community played with each other and talked about what we were going to be when we grew up. Everyone probably did that at some point. I can see myself walking the streets, daydreaming about what my future was going to be like. I remember saying I wanted four children just like my mom. I was a fighter and a go-getter. I used to always see myself out of the environment I was in. It doesn't matter where you start in life, but it matters where you finish. Your beginning does not have to be your ending. Just because your beginning was bad, it does not mean that your ending cannot be good. The end of a thing is better than its beginning (Ecclesiastes 7:8, KJV). Your latter shall be greater than your former! My beginning was not so good, and maybe yours wasn't either, but it doesn't mean that your ending is not going to be great. Every story doesn't end sad. I once preached a message that was titled, "This Is not How My Story Will End." Your story will not end in pain, defeat, or destruction. Your story will be used for God's glory. There are many who see your success, but they don't know the cost of your alabaster box. They don't know the price that you paid to get to where you are.

One particular night, my mom along with others were at a certain house. They were drinking and doing their thing. Some kind of way, my sister got burned on her leg, and no one knew it. From my understanding, the pipe of a wood heater fell on her leg. My sister and I left, and she kept complaining about her leg. She was crying and saying she could not walk. When we made it home, my stepdad saw her leg. She was rushed to the hospital and transferred to the children's hospital in Birmingham, where she was treated and remained in the hospital for a while. After that incident, my mom stopped drinking for a while because Alabama Department of Human Resources stepped in. Make no mistake about it—my mom and stepdad were very good and loving people. They did the best they could. We didn't have everything we wanted, but we had what we needed. Dad worked for the city driving tractors, and he did yard work in the community for well-known and respected citizens. Dad was more of a talker and a joker than mom was. Mom was shy, unless she was drinking. When she was tipsy, she was going to tell you everything she wanted you to know and then some. I once heard that a drunk man's speech is a sober man's truth.

My siblings and I went to church almost every Sunday. In the midst of the environment we grew up in, it did not stop us from going to church. Our childhood was not the best, but it was not the worst either. There are some things I thank God for allowing me to go through as a child and a teenager. Being brought up in a small town called Carrville taught me so much about perseverance, endurance, hardship, and determination. Our church was St. John Baptist Church. We had a lot of seasoned saints in the church. We learned songs like: *Soon and Very Soon We Are Going to See the King*, *This Little Light of Mine*,

Amazing Grace, *I'm Running for My Life*, and so many others. We said Christmas and Easter speeches. I was being trained in the ways of God in church. Proverbs 22:6 in the New King James Version tells us, "Train up a child in the way he should go, And when he is old he will not depart from it." I am now pastoring a church where children are in church plays, praise dances, and so much more. As I look back over my life, I can see that God was preparing me at an early age to be a leader in the same community I was born and raised in. As I am writing this book, chills are running through my body because I still cannot believe that God chose me. How grateful and humble I am to be his servant! Carrville is where I grew up. The section where my family lived was known for violence, crime, and toughness. Even though there were many good people who lived near us, other people knew not to mess with anyone from Carrville. From my understanding, the police were afraid to come to our neighborhood, which was down the hill. "'Can any good thing come out of Nazareth?' Nathanael asked. 'Come and see,' said Philip" (John 1:46, BSB).

It is sad to say that some people will try to label you because of the community that you live in, the car you drive, or the family you came from. Everyone is not the same. I have seen some of the most loving, respectful, and successful people come from some of the most remote communities. Never judge a book by its cover. There are many of us who were determined to make it out of the hood and make something out of ourselves. I'm from the hood, but I am just as good. It was the things that we went through that motivated us to want to do better in life. Generational curses can be broken. History does not have to repeat itself in a negative way. I dropped out of school and later went back to GED school and obtained my high school diploma. Eventually, I went to college and received a bachelor's degree in sociology. I broke a generational curse. All of my children graduated from high school; two of them are college graduates, and one is in college. The other one is pursuing acting and helping young adults overcome obstacles in life. I am not bragging or boasting by any means. My prayer is that you are inspired by my testimony and realize that if God did it for me, He will do the same thing for you because He is no respecter of persons (Acts 10:34).

"The journey may not be easy,
however, your reward at the end
will be worth it."

—OBVIOUS MAGAZINE

Chapter 5
The Journey Was Not Easy

Eventually, I moved out as a teenager because I thought I wanted to be grown. I am grateful for the three women who allowed me to stay with them during my teenage years. I will never forget their love and their act of kindness. As the older folk said, "a hard head will make a soft behind." I eventually learned much more about life, people, and the streets. I was headed for destruction, and no one could tell me anything because I thought I had this thing called life figured out. I didn't care who you were or how big or tall you were if you crossed me the wrong way, I would fight you. I found out the hard way that the way I was going was leading me to destruction. "There is a way that appears to be right, but in the end, it leads to death" (Proverbs 14:12, NIV). I was looking for love in all the wrong places. I was looking for love in too many faces. There was a void I was trying to fill in worldly pleasure. Merriam-Webster.com defines void as "an opening or gap, empty space, emptiness, vacuum, the quality or state of being without something, lack, absence." I was looking for something or someone to fill the emptiness I was feeling on the inside. There were so many things that I lacked as a child, a teenager, and an adult that only God was able to give. Maybe some of you can relate to my story. Maybe your childhood was not so good. Maybe you were abused, raped, molested, adopted, or abandoned. Maybe you did not get the love, support, attention, or praise that you longed for. Maybe you were always criticized, even when you tried your best. Maybe you were told that you would never amount to anything. I was told by others that I would never amount to anything, but look at God. Man does not determine your destiny, God does. It is not what man says about you; it's about what you say about yourself. I cancel every negative word that has been spoken over your life.

I had to learn that hurting people hurt other people. People cannot give you what they never had unless there is a divine transformation because I believe with God all things are possible. Some people can only love you the way they have been loved. Because of the environment I grew up in, I promised myself that I would always be there for my children and support them in school and all of their endeavors. I praised them, supported them, complimented them, and encouraged them. I failed in some areas and succeeded in others. The journey has not been easy, but it has been worth it. We must be willing to go through the process to get to the promise. Life is not always fair, and neither are people. If we let it mold us, make us, and shape us, we will come out victorious. Broken crayons still color! Just because you break a crayon it doesn't mean you throw it away. The crayon is still usable. Your life is still usable to God. God is not going to throw you away. Just because you came from a broken home or a broken family it doesn't mean that God cannot use you or that your life cannot be beautiful. There's beauty in your brokenness! God can take a broken vessel and make it whole again. God can take a broken family and make it whole again. God can take a broken marriage and make it whole again. God can take a broken heart and make it whole again. "Is there no balm in Gilead? Is there no physician there? Why then is there no healing for the wound of my people?" (Jeremiah 8:22, NIV). There is a balm in Gilead. God wants to heal your wounds. It is time out for putting a Band-Aid on a major wound. Michael Connelly stated, "You can't patch a wounded soul with a Band-Aid." You can't patch a wounded life, ministry, or relationship with a Band-Aid either. God is the Great Physician. He is a doctor in a sick room and a lawyer in a courtroom. He is Jehovah-Rapha, the God who heals you. This is your season to be healed, delivered, and set free! God is not done with you. He has a plan and a purpose for your life. God can take who the world called a nobody and make them a somebody. God will take the foolish thing from the world to confound the wise (1 Corinthians 1:27). Some relationships can be saved if we take the time to hear the conclusion of the whole matter. I had to go through spiritual healing, emotional healing, and mental healing. I had to make a decision to either let it make me bitter or make me better. I chose to become better. I had to take those lemons that life, people, and situations threw at me and make lemonade.

There are still people who can't believe that God has raised me up to be a leader because they know where I came from and what I've been through. Sometimes, I still cannot believe God chose a little, small-town girl like me. I am still in awe of His glorious work. I am a living testimony that God can save and deliver anybody. We all have a story to tell, and this is why I am telling mine. My life story has caused many to come and hear me preach. As a result of my preaching, many have accepted Jesus Christ as their personal Savior. If God calls you, He qualifies you. Many of you are probably like I was, feeling very unqualified to preach the gospel or do what God put on your heart to do. I never wanted to be a preacher, and I never asked to be a preacher. However, the call was very evident on my life. I had no choice but to surrender to God after I had a supernatural encounter with Him in my kitchen. I surrendered all. My life was on display. As God was raising me up as a leader, I was in spiritual therapy, and I didn't even know it. There were some old wounds that began to come to the surface. As I was preaching and declaring deliverance to others, there were things in my life I thought I was delivered from that began to surface. A lot of times, we think we have been delivered from certain things because we don't see the manifestations. However, when you are offended by someone and the things you thought you were delivered from begin to manifest, you ask yourself, "Where did that come from?" Maybe no one touched that old wound or that part of you in a while.

I have always been a happy and joyful person, but I was easily offended in my early days because of things I felt were not right. The Bible says, "And with all thy getting get understanding" (Proverbs 4:7, KJV). I had to learn that just because I felt like something was not right, it did not mean the person's intentions were not right. Not all intentions were well, but not all were bad either. I had to take the good with the bad. I must be honest and say I made some mistakes myself. Sometimes, my judgment was off, but my intentions were well. We must listen to understand. I took the stumbling blocks that the enemy put in my path and used them as my steppingstones. The enemy thought that I was going to trip and fall, but I stepped right on up to my next level. Sometimes, you are going to have some bitter experiences, but it doesn't mean you have to become bitter.

"Let your past
make you BETTER,
and not bitter."

−UNKNOWN

Chapter 6

Don't Let Life Make You Bitter But Better

Life presented Naomi with some bitter experiences. "Don't call me Naomi," she responded. "Instead, call me Mara, for the Almighty has made life very bitter for me" (Ruth 1:20, NLT). Naomi lost her husband and her two sons. All she had was her two daughters-in-law, Ruth and Orpah. Orpah went back to Moab. People who are not connected to you will go back. Nothing or no one can keep people who don't want to stay from leaving. Nothing or no one can make people who want to stay leave. Ruth was all the way in. Loyalty is proven in tough times. It was easy for Orpah to leave because she was not all the way in. Ruth remained loyal and connected to her mother-in-law to the very end. She was in for the long haul.

I want people in my life who are going to be with me whether I am up or down. I want some people who are going to ride the bus with me when the limousine breaks down. I don't know about you, but I think everything that Naomi went through would have made her become a bitter old woman, but the Bible doesn't say she was a bitter person. It says she said to call her Mara because the Almighty had dealt very bitterly with her. She had some bitter experiences, but she was not bitter. There are some people who can go through some storms in life and choose not to become bitter. Charles R. Swindoll said, "Life is 10% what happens to you and 90% how you react to it." Every action doesn't need a reaction. Just because someone kills your cat, it doesn't mean you have to kill their dog. "Vengeance is mine, I will repay, says the Lord" (Romans 12:19, ESV). We should never take matters into our own hands. Many of us know people who have sought revenge on their adversary or someone who has caused them pain, and the end result was destruction for the one who sought revenge. "Do not be overcome by evil, but overcome evil with good" (Romans 12:21, NIV). There have been times in my life where people have plotted, conspired, and falsely accused me of things that I knew were false. I must admit that I was hurt, broken, and lost for words, but I never did to them what they did to me. As a matter of fact, in return, I helped them. Even though some bad things happened to me as a child, a teenager, and an adult, it doesn't mean I have to walk around with a victim's mentality. Also, it doesn't mean that I want to get those people back who hurt me or offended me. Some things that occurred in my life were because of the poor choices that I made, and I had to suffer the consequences. There were some people who were in my life that God told me to let go of, but because I wanted to help them and they were hurting me, it caused me much pain. We have to take responsibility for our own actions. I had to acknowledge that everything was not the devil. We give the enemy too much credit sometimes. James 4:7, ESV says, "Submit yourselves therefore to God. Resist the devil, and he will flee from you." The Merriam-Webster dictionary defines submit as "to yield oneself to the authority or will of another." We must yield our members unto the Lord. We must resist and fight back with the word of God, and Satan will flee or run from us. We cannot afford to give the enemy a foothold in our lives because a foothold will become a stronghold. If you give him an inch, he will take a mile. If you let him ride, he is going to want to drive. We must deny him access into our lives by sealing all of the cracks and holes with the word of God. We must be aware of the enemy's plan, so that he will not have an advantage over us. If someone made you aware that there was a snake in your bed, would you still get in it? Knowledge is powerful, but knowledge without wisdom is dangerous. Hosea 4:6, says, "My people are destroyed for lack of knowledge." What you do not know can destroy you. A known enemy is a defeated enemy! When you are aware of his plans, plots, and schemes, you have an advantage. The weapon may have formed against you, but it did not prosper. If it had prospered in your life, you would not be reading this book. You are an overcomer! You are victorious!

"So if the Son sets you free,
you are truly free."

—JOHN 8:36, NLT

Chapter 7

Free Indeed

Luke 8:1-2 in the Berean Study Bible says, "Soon afterward, Jesus traveled from one town and village to another, preaching and proclaiming the good news of the kingdom of God. The Twelve were with Him, as well as some women who had been healed of evil spirits and infirmities: Mary called Magdalene, from whom seven demons had gone out, Joanna the wife of Herod's household manager Chuza, Susanna, and many others. These women were ministering to them out of their own means." These women had been healed, delivered, and set free. As a result of being healed, delivered, and set free, in return, they supported the ministry of Jesus with their means. They showed gratefulness and appreciation by supporting the very ministry of Jesus. They knew where their deliverance and healing came from. I can hear them saying, "I once was lost, but now I am found. I once was blind, but now I see. I once was bound, but now I am free. I once was sick, but now I am healed." I can only imagine how these women of God felt after receiving their healing from Jesus. I can speak from experience. When Jesus delivered me and set me free, I wanted the whole world to know what the Lord had done for me. When you have a life-changing experience with the Lord, it is impossible to keep it to yourself. I wanted everyone to know about my Lord and Savior. I wanted to do whatever I could to help advance the kingdom of God. It was in my heart to serve in any capacity I could as an act of gratitude. I don't see how we can have a supernatural encounter with the Lord and not be a blessing to others. When you know that it was the Lord who saved you, delivered you, and brought you out, you just can't keep it to yourself. You have to tell somebody how good the Lord has been to you.

The woman at the well could not keep the good news to herself either. "And he must needs go through Samaria. Then cometh he to a city of Samaria, which is called Sychar, near to the parcel of ground that Jacob gave to his son Joseph. Now Jacob's well was there. Jesus therefore, being wearied with his journey, sat thus on the well: and it was about the sixth hour. There cometh a woman of Samaria to draw water: Jesus saith unto her, Give me to drink. (For his disciples were gone away unto the city to buy meat.) Then saith the woman of Samaria unto him, How is it that thou, being a Jew, askest drink of me, which am a woman of Samaria? for the Jews have no dealings with the Samaritans. Jesus answered and said unto her, If thou knewest the gift of God, and who it is that saith to thee, Give me to drink; thou wouldest have asked of him, and he would have given thee living water. The woman saith unto him, Sir, thou hast nothing to draw with, and the well is deep: from whence then hast thou that living water?" (John 4:4-11, KJV). There was a need for Jesus to go through Samaria. This Samaritan woman went to the well at noon. Could it be that she was trying to avoid the other women in her community because of her previous relationships? In my opinion, twelve noon was probably too hot to draw water from a well. Or could it have been her spot to meet other men? I wonder if she was really going to the well to get water, or was she using the water pot as a cover up? I think you would go early in the morning or late in the evening because it was cooler especially if it was summer. However, Jesus showed up at noon. I believe it was intentional. Jesus asked her for a drink. She said He didn't have anything to draw with, and the well was deep. I wonder do we have people coming to our churches and we don't have anything to draw them with. People are in some deep stuff, and it is going to take the Spirit of God and the anointing to draw them. Deep calleth unto deep. We must be willing to launch out into the deep. This Samaritan woman had a divine appointment. It was a setup from Jesus. She was about to have a life-changing experience with her seventh husband. This woman's life was about to be complete. I believe this woman at the well was looking for love in all the wrong places. She was looking for love in too many faces. Nevertheless, she was about to be made whole. She may have gone to the well to draw water, but Jesus ended up drawing her. She may have gone to the well for one thing, but she left with another thing. She may have gone to the well thirsty for natural water, but she left filled with the living water. She was so excited about her encounter, salvation, and life-changing experience with Jesus that she left her water pot and ran into the city and told the men of that city about a man that she had met that told her everything that she had done. She said, "Come, see a man who told me everything I ever did. Could this be the Messiah?" (John 4:29, NIV). This woman became a witness for Jesus. She could not keep the good news to herself. She wanted others to know about the man that told her everything.

I know exactly how she felt. When Jesus saved me, I wanted the whole world to know that I was saved, and I wanted everyone to be saved. You cannot keep the good news to yourself. I felt something I had never felt in my life. I felt a peace that surpasses all understanding. I felt unspeakable joy. I felt so much love. Just like this woman left her water pot, I left the streets, the clubs, and my old lifestyle because Jesus got to the root cause of my problems.

Can I keep it real? Jesus got all in her business! Did you catch that? There have been many people who have asked me and others, "How do you know my business?" They have asked others if they told me what they were going through. Some have even said they were afraid to come to my church because they did not want to be called out. God reveals to redeem. Jesus said to her, "Go, call your husband, and come here." The woman answered him, "I have no husband." Jesus said to her, "You are right in saying, 'I have no husband';

for you have had five husbands, and the one you now have is not your husband. What you have said is true" (John 4:16-18, ESV). Jesus got down to the nitty gritty. He didn't sugarcoat it or beat around the bush. He called it like He saw it. Jesus got all the way down to the root cause of this woman's relationship problems.

When I think about this woman's life, I am reminded how so many of us go from one relationship to the next, without being healed from the previous relationship. If we are always jumping in and out of dysfunctional relationships, we will continue to have conflict in our current relationship. There has to be healing and closure from your previous relationship. If not, you are more likely to have some of the same issues in your next relationship. If there was abuse, infidelity, and unresolved conflict, it's very important that you give yourself the proper time to heal. I have seen people come out of a toxic relationship and become angry and bitter because of how they were mistreated and abused. And when they started dating someone who really loved them unconditionally, they had trust issues, or they did not know how to accept and receive love from their significant other because of the way they had been mistreated.

Being single is not going to kill you and being married is not going to heal you. We must allow ourselves the proper time to heal mentally, emotionally, and spiritually. Jesus had what it took to draw the woman at the well out. Jesus has what it takes to draw you out too. I don't know what you are in that is deep, that makes you feel as if no one has what it takes to get you out. You are not reading this book by chance, coincidence, or accident. Jesus has what it takes to draw you out, pull you out, and get you out. Psalm 40:2 in the New International Version encourages, "He lifted me out of the slimy pit, out of the mud and mire; he set my feet on a rock and gave me a firm place to stand." You will never know what it is like to be stuck in a slimy pit, mud, and mire unless you have been in it. I can recall being in a car that was stuck in mud, and the more you tried to get it out, the more the wheels spun around. You could see the mud all over the tires of the car as a result of the car being stuck in mud. Some of us were like a car stuck in some slimy and muddy situations, and the more you tried to get out, the more you kept going around in circles. Maybe it seems as if you were sinking in quicksand. Maybe you were stuck in a relationship that kept taking you around and around. Maybe your head and your emotions kept spinning. Maybe you kept going in circles. There is a song that says, "You got me going in circles, round and round I go." Maybe the woman at the well was stuck in a relationship that was not going anywhere. Perhaps she had been going in circles, but Jesus showed up to break the cycle!

Your days of going in circles are over! This is not the season to keep going back and forth with anyone. You have to know your worth and value because if you don't, you will settle for anything and anybody. I believe that the woman's life was just as empty as the pot she was carrying. And when you are thirsty for a relationship, thirsty for success, thirsty for ministry, you have to be careful who you drink from. I believe this woman at the well was spiritually thirsty, and Jesus had what it took to quench her thirst. "Jesus answered her, "If you knew the gift of God and who it is that asks you for a drink, you would have asked him and he would have given you living water." "Sir," the woman said, "you have nothing to draw with and the well is deep. Where can you get this living water? Are you greater than our father Jacob, who gave us the well and drank from it himself, as did also his sons and his livestock?" Jesus answered, "Everyone who drinks this water will be thirsty again, but whoever drinks the water I give them will never thirst. Indeed, the water I give them will become in them a spring of water welling up to eternal life." The woman said to him, "Sir, give me this water so that I won't get thirsty and have to keep coming here to draw water" (John 4:10-15, NIV). There were many times when I was a child, my mom would ask me to go get water for the house. I could not get polluted water because she was going to cook, clean, and wash with it. I knew to get the water from the city's faucet that was near our house. The water could not be contaminated. You can't drink from every cup that is offered to you. That is how you get poisoned.

God is about to deliver you, so you don't have to keep doing the same thing over and over. Even if she did not get the full understanding and revelation that was flowing from Jesus concerning the water, she still asked. Maybe you feel excluded and not included. Maybe you feel like an outcast and an outlaw. Maybe you feel like you have been so bad or have made so many mistakes that God cannot save you and deliver you. God doesn't look at your past to determine your future.

"Your history does not need to define your destiny."

―CHRISTINE CAINE

Chapter 8

Your Past Doesn't Define You

Jesus came to seek and save those who were lost. Jesus did not come to call the righteous. He came that sinners may repent. Those who are sick, they need a physician. Yesterday is history, today is a gift, and tomorrow is a mystery. "Therefore, if any man be in Christ Jesus, he is a new creature. Old things are passed away; and behold, all things are become new" (2 Corinthians 5:17, KJV). It doesn't matter where you start in life, but what matters is how you finish. Your past is your past. You don't live there anymore. When the devil tries to throw up your past, you remind him of his future. There is no double jeopardy in the kingdom. While we were yet sinners, Christ died for us. If you have accepted Jesus Christ as your Lord and Savior and repented for your sins, you are saved. According to Romans 10:9, NIV, "If you declare with your mouth, 'Jesus is Lord,' and believe in your heart that God raised him from the dead, you will be saved." This woman was asking for something that only Jesus could give her, and that was salvation and eternal life. John 14:6 in the New Living Translation says, "I am the way, the truth, and the life. No one can come to the Father except through me." God's word is a road map that will lead you to eternal life. I can recall getting lost while traveling because I didn't know the way, so I had to ask someone who knew the way. They gave me the direction that led me to my destination. This woman was lost, but when she met Jesus, she received information and direction on how to get on the right road, which was eternal life. If you are on the wrong path, I pray that this book will help you get on the right path.

There is salvation in no one else! God has given no other name under heaven by which we must be saved. This lady is a great example of how we must go through Christ to receive salvation. Jesus Christ is the one who laid down His life for all mankind. This woman was hungry and thirsty for the truth, and on that day, her spirit was filled. She was so full that she could not keep it to herself. She received the overflow. "In the last day, that great day of the feast, Jesus stood and cried, saying, If any man thirst, let him come unto me, and drink. He that believeth on me, as the scripture hath said, out of his belly shall flow rivers of living water" (John 7:37-38, KJV). Her spiritual hunger was filled with the bread of life that came down from heaven above.

In the natural when you are hungry and thirsty, you eat and drink to satisfy your natural appetite. In the spiritual, you must read the word of God to feed your spiritual man. Jesus said, "Man shall not live by bread alone, but by every word that proceedeth out of the mouth of God" (Matthew 4:4, KJV). The word of God is our daily bread and our weapon. We say, "An apple a day will help keep the doctor away." Also, a scripture a day will help keep the devil away.

"God is glorified through healing and deliverance, not through sickness and suffering."

―KENNETH E. HAGIN

Chapter 9
Deliverance Is Coming to Your House

Ephesians 6:11 in the King James Version declares, "Put on the whole armour of God, that ye may be able to stand against the wiles of the devil." Wiles is defined in the *Cambridge English Dictionary* as "ways of persuading someone that trick them into doing something and skill and ways of tricking people into doing what you want." In Genesis the second chapter, it was a serpent that tricked Eve into eating the forbidden fruit. I know firsthand what it feels like to be tricked, deceived, and manipulated by the enemy. The enemy is very cunning, crafty, sneaky, and conniving. We must be wise as serpents and harmless as doves. It is very imperative that we watch as well as pray, so we do not become the enemy's prey.

Jesus was anointed to set the captives free! Acts 10:38 in the King James Version states,

"Now God anointed Jesus of Nazareth with the Holy Ghost and with power: who went about doing good, and healing all that were oppressed of the devil; for God was with him." There are many people who attend our churches, who go in and come out the same way they went in because there is no anointing or power in our churches. According to Isaiah 10:27, it is the anointing that destroys the yoke. Jesus had a deliverance, healing, and miracle ministry. "The reason the Son of God appeared was to destroy the devil's work" (1 John 3:8, NIV). One instance when Jesus destroyed such works is evident in the following passage of scripture. "When Jesus arrived at the other side of the lake in the area of the Gadarene people, two men who had demons in them met him. These men lived in the burial caves and were so dangerous that people could not use the road by those caves. They shouted, "What do you want with us, Son of God? Did you come here to torture us before the right time?" Near that place there was a large herd of pigs feeding. The demons begged Jesus, "If you make us leave these men, please send us into that herd of pigs." Jesus said to them, "Go!" So the demons left the men and went into the pigs. Then the whole herd rushed down the hill into the lake and were drowned" (Matthew 8:28-32, NCV). The spirit of death and destruction were after these two men, but Jesus and His disciples went through a major storm to get to them. You never know what someone had to go through to get to you. You will never know the price or the sacrifices that were made to get you delivered and set free. You will never know the cost, the pain, the suffering, the sleepless nights, the fasting, and the prayers that were made on you and your family's behalf. The reason you are still here is because someone prayed for you. We used to sing a song that said, *"Somebody prayed for me, Happy I must be, They took the time and prayed for me."*

The spirits that were living in these men were so dangerous that people were afraid of them. People avoided traveling that road because they were afraid of these men because of the demons that were manifesting through them. These two men were living by the tombs. Evil spirits were controlling these men. These evil spirits knew who Jesus was just like they know who we are. These men were not in their right mind just like some of us when we were under demonic controls or possessed by evil spirits that had us doing things we would never have done if we had been in our right mind. I am so glad that Jesus heard their cry. There is nothing too hard for God! These men had the entire town in fear, but Jesus confronted the evil spirits and cast them out. They asked to go into the herds, and Jesus said, "Go," and they entered into the pigs and drowned themselves. No doubt, those evil spirits wanted these men to hurt themselves, hurt someone else, or commit suicide, but God! These men experienced a mighty deliverance through the ministry of Jesus Christ. No wonder hell was mad, and heaven was glad because someone showed up on the scene to set the captives free. Jesus was a mover, a shaker, and a history maker. These men were delivered and set free. They were clothed in their right minds! The entire town came out to see Jesus. When you do something that has never been done before, people will either be glad or mad. They pleaded with Jesus to leave their town. Some people don't want you around when you bring deliverance to others because they can no longer control them. However, I believe the reason they wanted Jesus to leave was because the pigs ran into the lake and drowned themselves. They were more focused on a profit than souls being delivered and set free. I think they should have asked him to stay. If someone came into my town and set these men free I would have pleaded with him to stay. I don't know if they were afraid, but it sure would have increased my faith to see that kind of deliverance and liberation. These men were healed from mental, emotional, and psychological torment, physical pain, violent outbursts, and so much more. What they were feeling on the inside was manifesting on the outside. So many people are like these men at the tombs. They are being tormented by evil and demonic spirits, and they are only acting out what they feel on the inside. There is a reason that people do what they do. I know that everything is not a spirit or a devil. One thing I know for sure is that if you have done everything that you possibly can and things have not changed but have grown worse, you probably need deliverance. You can't counsel a devil. It has to be cast out!

These men were healed and restored back to their original state. Restore is defined in the Merriam-Webster.com dictionary as "to bring back to or put back into a former or original state." If you are wondering if things will ever get back to normal in your life, I have good news for you. When you have done your best, let God do the rest. Your life is not over. Your future is not over.

God is not done with you. There may be people who say they are done with you, but the Lord is saying, "I am just now getting started. Your family will be saved! Your family will be healed! Your family will be restored!" Whatever you do, don't stop believing. Never give up! Never stop believing and trusting in the Lord. He is a present help in the time of a storm.

"You can't go back and change the beginning, but you can start where you are and change the ending."

—C. S. LEWIS

Chapter 10

A Change Is Going to Come

Job said, "I am going to wait until my change comes." In the midst of everything that Job went through, he waited until his change came. I am talking about a man who lost all of his wealth, his children, and to top it off, he was afflicted with boils, but he still kept the faith. Through it all, we must learn how to trust in the Lord. In the end, God gave Job double for all of his trouble. According to the King James Version of Job 42:10, "God turned the captivity of Job when he prayed for his friends: also the Lord gave Job twice as much as he had before." Can you pray for someone who has falsely accused you? Can you pray for someone who has lied on you? Can you pray for someone who has hurt you? There have been many people who I have had to pray for who have lied on me, talked about me, falsely accused me, and slandered my name. We all go through certain things in life. Sometimes, we have to let people think what they want to think about us, and we must stop trying to explain ourselves to people who are committed to misunderstanding us. Just because someone is sick or they lose their job, house, car, or other items it does not mean they have done something wrong. Some people have the tendency to think that karma has knocked on your door, or you are reaping what you have sowed. That is not always the case. Sometimes, it is because of what you are doing right. Psalm 34:19 in the New King James Version says, "Many are the afflictions of the righteous: but the LORD delivereth him out of them all."

Job was a righteous man, one who feared God and stayed away from evil. He was the greatest of all mankind of the east, but it did not stop him from suffering. You can fear God and stay away from evil, but it doesn't mean that evil will stay away from you. Paul said, "When I try to do good, evil is always present" (Romans 7:21).

There is only so much that the enemy can do. There was a hedge of protection around Job's house. "Have you not put a hedge around him and his household and everything he has? You have blessed the work of his hands, so that his flocks and herds are spread throughout the land. But now stretch out your hand and strike everything he has, and he will surely curse you to your face." The Lord said to Satan, "Very well, then, everything he has is in your power, but on the man himself do not lay a finger" (Job 1:10-12, NIV). As I read this story over, I realized that God knew that Job was living right. He knew he was upright, and he did not have anything to do with evil. In other words, he avoided evil at all cost. God knew that Job reverenced him. God knew that Job respected him and honored him. I believe that Satan had been checking Job out as well because he knew that God had put a hedge of protection around Job's house, his household, and his possessions. He knew that God had blessed the work of Job's hands. He had checked out his wealth, his children, his wife, his servants, his sheep, his camels, his oxen, and his female donkeys. I believe that the enemy was using all of these things as an avenue to Job's faith. What the enemy fails to realize is that Job's faith in God was stronger than the adversity, misfortune, disaster, calamity, sorrow, grief, pain, and suffering. Job puts it this way, "Naked I came from my mother's womb, and naked I will depart.

The Lord gave and the Lord has taken away; may the name of the Lord be praised" (Job 1:21, NIV).

The enemy never expected Job to praise God in the midst of the storm. In the midst of the storm, praise your way through, even when you can't see your way through. God will come through. The Bible says, "If thou faint in the day of adversity, your strength is small" (Proverbs 24:10, KJV). Faith that has not been tested cannot be trusted. There is victory in your praise. When you praise, you get raised. When you complain, you remain. Your praise will confuse the enemy. Don't you think for one second that the enemy is not checking you, your family, your spouse, and your possessions out. He wants to hit you where it hurts the most. Your faith has to be in God and not things. Maybe that is why you are going through with your children, your family, your spouse, your health, and your finances. He wants you to deny Christ. If you will just stand the test of time, you will come out victorious in the end. The enemy is trying to weaken your faith in the Lord. Job's faith was unshakeable! His faith was tried by fire, but he came out as pure gold. In the end, Job came out better than ever. His health was restored. He was blessed with seven sons and three daughters, and the daughters looked better than the first ones. He received double for all of his trouble! His sisters, brothers, and acquaintances came and blessed him. There are people who saw you going through who are going to witness you coming out. They will see that it was the Lord who kept you and brought you out. God is going to make it up to you!

"The words you speak
will become
your reality."

−JOEL OSTEEN

Chapter 11
Speak the Word

God wants to heal you everywhere you hurt. Life and death are in the power of your tongue. You can have whatsoever you say. The Bible says in Job 22:28, "Thou shalt also decree a thing, and it shall be established unto thee: and the light shall shine upon thy ways." There are some things that you can speak into existence. There have been times in my life, when I have spoken healing and blessings into existence. As a true believer, you have the authority to decree and declare. "He sent his word, and healed them, and delivered them from their destructions" (Psalm 107:20, KJV). There were times when Jesus spoke the word, and the word brought forth healing. There will be times when you will have to speak it until you see it. The centurion answered and said, "Lord, I am not worthy that thou shouldest come under my roof: but speak the word only, and my servant shall be healed" (Matthew 8:8, KJV). The centurion had enough faith to believe that if Jesus would just speak the word, his servant would be made whole. Sometimes, you may not be able to go to the hospital, jail, or school, but if you just speak the word, it shall be done. We go on to see in Isaiah 55:11 God says, "So shall my word be that goeth forth out of my mouth: it shall not return unto me void." You can send the word to the hospital, school, or jail, and that word will not return back unto you void, but it will accomplish the purpose for which it was sent. It will hit the bull's-eye.

There have been times when people sent for me, and I was not always able to go, but I sent the word, and the word brought forth healing, deliverance, and a breakthrough. "For the word of God is quick and powerful, and sharper than any two-edged sword" (Hebrews 4:12, KJV). When you speak the word, it has the power to travel to the person that you sent it to. The word of God has quickening power. No matter what it is that you are facing in life, you have to have enough faith to believe that God has the power to heal you and save you. "Heal me, O Lord, and I shall be healed; save me, and I shall be saved, for you are my praise" (Jeremiah 17:14, ESV). We praise

Him for what He has done, and we worship Him for who He is.

This is your season to be healed from the wounds of your past and the things in life that have cut you so deeply on the inside and that are keeping you up all night (Psalm 147:3). There are things preventing you from moving forward in life. It is time to admit yourself into God's care, so you can receive your divine healing. The internal bleeding stops now! The spiritual hemorrhaging stops now! I don't know if you were broken when you picked this book up, but before you put it down, you will be made whole. God is going to put the broken pieces back together in your life. Maybe your life has been like a puzzle scattered all over the place, but by the time God starts putting the pieces together, you will see the whole picture. God is putting your life back together. The potter wants to put you back together again.

The dry bones were scattered everywhere in Ezekiel 37. They were in an open valley. Have you ever gone through anything in the open? Have you suffered in the open? Have you had a crisis in the open? God asked Ezekiel, "Can these dry bones live?" Ezekiel said, "Lord, you know" (Ezekiel 37:3). God told Ezekiel to prophesy to the dry bones. The prophet prophesied to the dry bones, and they came together, bone to bone. He prophesied to the four winds, and the wind from all four directions came and breathed upon the slain, and they stood up on their feet and became a great army (Ezekiel 37:7-10). They represented the house of Israel. What was dead, God brought back to life. God is about to bring back to life what's been pronounced dead in your life, family, destiny, and ministry. God is about to breathe on your ministry, breathe on your destiny, breathe on your marriage, and breathe on your family. The things that have been scattered are about to come together. The members that have been scattered are about to come together. The Body of Christ is about to come together. Family members are about to come together.

The bones were dry, and no life was in them. There are many people who are dry, and there is no spirit in them. They are void of the presence of God. There are churches that are dry. There are people who speak to you who are dry. They are spiritually dead. There is no fire or glory in the church. There are churches that are cold. They feel like a morgue instead of a church. The word of God brings life. We need prophetic revelation in our churches. "Surely the Sovereign Lord does nothing without revealing his plan to his servants the prophets" (Amos 3:7, NIV). We must bring back the fire and the glory of God to our churches. It is time to prophesy to the dry bones and tell them to hear the word of God. Where God is, there is life. Where God is, there is love! Where God is, there is hope! Where God is, there is deliverance! Where God is, there is light! Where God is, there is healing, forgiveness, restoration, and truth. Where God is, there is liberty (2 Corinthians 3:17). So if the Son sets you free, you will be free indeed (John 8:36, NIV).

"I've learned that people will forget what you said, people will forget what you did, but people will never forget how you made them feel."

−MAYA ANGELOU

Chapter 12

One Touch

If you have the glory, people will find you. That's for sure. Let's look at Jesus, for example. "Great crowds came to him, bringing the lame, the blind, and the crippled, the mute and many others, and laid them at his feet; and he healed them" (Matthew 15:30, NIV). Jesus's fame spread abroad because of his deliverance, healing, and miracle ministry. The blind received their sight. The lame walked. The dumb talked. The deaf ears were opened, and the dead were raised. People brought all their sick to him and begged him to let the sick just touch the edge of his cloak, and all who touched it were healed (Matthew 14:35-36, NIV).

The anointing is tangible and transferable. We see this in Luke 8:43-48, KJV. "And a woman having an issue of blood twelve years, which had spent all of her living upon physicians, neither could be healed of any, came behind him, and touched the border of his garment: and immediately her issue of blood stanched. And Jesus said, who touched me? When all denied, Peter and they that were with him said, Master, the multitude throng thee and press thee, and sayest thou, who touched me? And Jesus said, Somebody hath touched me: for I perceive that virtue is gone out of me. And when the woman saw that she was not hid, she came trembling, and falling down before him, she declared unto him before all the people for what cause she had touched him, and how she was healed immediately. And he said unto her, Daughter, be of good comfort: thou faith hath made thee whole; go in peace."

The woman with the issue of blood had suffered for twelve long years, and she was considered unclean because of her condition. "When a woman has her regular flow of blood, the impurity of her monthly period will last seven days, and anyone who touches her will be unclean till evening" (Leviticus 15:19, NIV). This woman had enough faith, courage, and determination to break the Jewish law to receive her healing. In spite of what she felt inside of her body, she pressed her way. The Bible says that she said within herself, "If I may but touch his garment, I shall be whole." Sometimes, you have to say it to yourself, speak to yourself, pray for yourself, encourage yourself, and believe in yourself. She didn't say, "If He touches me, I will be whole." She said if she could only touch the hem of His garment, she would be made whole. There was a member of my church who has gone home to be with the Lord. She was blind but had crazy faith. She once told me that if she couldn't make it to church but if she could only touch the red string of a piece of bologna, she knew that she would be made whole. Maybe you can't understand the significance of the red bologna string, so let me help you understand. I believe this awesome mother of Zion saw the bologna string as the blood of Jesus. Even though she did not have natural sight, she saw in the spirit. Helen Keller said, "The only thing worse than being blind is having sight but no vision." This mother of Zion didn't have sight, but she had vision. I would like to liken the red bologna string to Rahab's scarlet thread that was used in her window as a reminder to spare her house and her family. I believe that the scarlet thread represented the blood of Jesus. And because of her act of faith and obedience, her family was spared. Too many times, we are waiting on someone to call us up for prayer, lay hands on us, or prophesy to us so we can receive our healing. When the healing anointing is flowing, you can receive your healing without anyone laying their hands on you. This woman came from behind, pressed her way through the crowd, and touched the hem of Jesus's garment, and at that very moment, she was made whole. She had spent everything that she had, going to doctor after doctor, but she did not get any better but grew worse. Isn't it amazing how she suffered for twelve long years and spent all that she had going back and forth to the doctor and never got any better, but things grew worse? She had an issue of blood. She had an issue with her blood that created a flow. Did you get that? She had an issue that created a flow. Some of us started out with one thing that created another thing. She had this flow for twelve long years. I don't know what your issue is, but God is about to deal with it. The flow of problems stops now! This is a new day, and you will no longer have to go back and forth to the doctor, back and forth to the jailhouse, or back and forth in that relationship. Your days of going through the same things are over! She had suffered for twelve years, and she was healed in one day!

As you are reading this book, I decree and declare that this is your day! Today is your day! It's a new day! She got something that her money could not buy. Sometimes, it seems as if things get worse before they get better. They will get better if you will keep the faith. The doctors could not get the glory. The Lord was the one who got the glory. Whatever this woman had heard about Jesus helped to activate her faith because she had enough faith to get up and get in the crowd in spite of how she felt. She knew within herself that if she could only touch the hem of his garment, she would be made whole. She was weak and feeble, but it did not stop her from pressing her way. She didn't make an excuse. She made an effort, and because of her determination, she received her healing. After she touched the hem of his garment, she knew within herself she was made whole. I think it is safe to say she felt that thing. There is something about when you know that you know. I will never forget how I suffered for many years with my sinuses. It got to the point that I had to receive shots because of the severity of it. I remember attending a revival one night, and I received my healing. It felt like heat went up my nostrils, and at that very moment, I knew

I was healed. To this day, I have not suffered with sinuses. To God be the glory!

The virtue that was in Jesus went into this woman. "Who touched me?" Jesus asked. When they all denied, Peter said, "Master, the people are crowding and pressing against you." But Jesus said, "Someone touched me; I know that power has gone out from me" (Luke 8:45-46, NIV). This woman put a demand on the anointing. She reached out and pulled it in. She made a withdrawal. I often think about all of the people who were around that anointing and didn't have a clue about what transpired. Is it that we can become so familiar with the anointing that we no longer benefit from it? Jesus and the woman knew that something happened. "Then the woman, seeing that she could not go unnoticed, came trembling and fell at his feet. In the presence of all the people, she told why she had touched him and how she had been instantly healed" (Luke 8:47, NIV).

What are you hoping for? What are you believing God for? What are you praying for? "Now faith is the substance of things hoped for, and the evidence of things not seen" (Hebrews 11:1, KJV). Trust God even when you can't trace God. "For we walk by faith and not by sight" (2

Corinthians 5:7, New KJV). We as believers have to believe it before we see it. It is called blind faith. When God told me to write this book, I wrote it by faith. There were many voices running through my head, trying to convince me not to go through with it. As a believer, I had to chose faith over fear. "Now without faith it is impossible to please God, for the one who draws near to Him must believe that He exists and rewards those who seek Him" (Hebrews 11:6, HCSB). In this season of your life, be of good courage because your faith is going to make you whole. You can go to church in peace. You can go home in peace. You can go to work in peace. You will no longer have to suffer the way you suffered in the past. You will no longer have to be isolated because of your past. You will no longer be considered unclean but a daughter or a son. Your days of being ostracized are over. I can only imagine how this woman felt in her body after she received her healing. There had to be so much joy and peace knowing that she had finally received her healing. This is the only story that I read in the New Testament of a woman with an issue of blood for twelve years. Could there have been others? Was she the only one who had enough faith and courage to break the Jewish law to get her healing? One thing is for sure, she got a storyline. Her life is a testimony to other women who have suffered with an issue of blood, letting them know that if He did it for her, He will do the same thing for you. She got just what she wanted from the Lord.

There is a woman in my church who had suffered for a year with an issue of blood. She was told that she was going to have to have a hysterectomy, but she stood on the word of God. I prayed for her twice, and the second time, she said that when I laid my hands on her belly, she felt fire in her abdomen. God healed her body, and she did not need surgery. The flow stopped! To this very day, she is healed. We serve a miracle-working God.

"Remember every miracle in the Bible started with a really BIG problem."

—UNKNOWN

Chapter 13

He Is a Miracle Worker

You do not have to be a preacher for signs and wonders to follow you. If you are a true believer, there should be some signs following your life. They say that the proof is in the pudding. The word says, "And these signs shall follow them that believe; In my name shall they cast out devils; they shall speak with new tongues; They shall take up serpents; and if they drink any deadly thing, it shall not hurt them; they shall lay hands on the sick, and they shall recover" (Mark 16:17-18, KJV). Matthew 11:5, NIV says, "The blind receive sight, the lame walk, those who have leprosy are cleansed, the deaf hear, the dead are raised, and the good news is proclaimed to the poor." I can honestly say that signs and wonders are following my ministry. I have seen God heal the sick, cast out devils, open supernatural doors, and so much more. Jesus himself proclaimed, "Verily, verily, I say unto you, He that believeth on me, the works that I do shall he do also; and greater works than these shall he do; because I go unto my father" (John 14:12, KJV). When Jesus walked the earth, He could only be at one place at a time. However, Jesus now lives in every true believer, which means that He can be in more than one place at the same time. I can be in Alabama performing miracles in His name, and you can be in California performing miracles in His name.

Miracles is defined in the Merriam-Webster online dictionary as "an extraordinary event manifesting divine intervention in human affairs." Miracles did not die when Jesus was crucified. We see this in Acts 19:11-12, KJV. "And God wrought special miracles by the hands of Paul: So that from his body were brought unto the sick handkerchiefs or aprons, and the diseases departed from them, and the evil spirits went out of them." Just as God performed miracles by the hands of Paul, I have witnessed the Lord performing miracles in my ministry. I have seen God do the miraculous in our church. I believe in miracles! Mark 9:23 confirms the need to believe. "Jesus said unto him, if thou canst believe, all things are possible to him that believeth."

It is according to our faith. We cannot put a limit on what God can do. There is no failure in God! If we believe that God can save us, we should believe that He can heal us. God is able! "Now to him that is able to do exceedingly abundantly above all that we ask or think, according to the power that worketh in us" (Ephesians 3:20, KJV). God wants to exceed your expectations. He wants to give you a mind-boggling blessing.

"One who lives in a glass house, shouldn't cast stones. The more stones you throw; the greater risk you take of shattering everything around you. Once the wall is cracked, it will just get bigger, until it makes everything fall."

—UNKNOWN

Chapter 14

He that Is Without Sin Cast the First Stone

The woman who was caught in the very act of committing adultery was brought to Jesus by the religious leaders. They brought the woman, but they did not bring the man. These were men who understood the law to the fullest. I have no clue why they were covering up for the man. I often wonder if it could be that they knew the man? Was he one of their buddies? I know that the Bible says they were trying to trap Jesus. Have you ever had someone who tried to trap you, shame you, expose you, and they were guilty of the same thing, or they had some skeletons in their closets? They had some dirty laundry themselves. Matthew 7:1-3 in the King James Version reiterates this. "Judge not, that ye be not judged. For with what judgement ye judge, ye shall be judged: and with what measure ye mete, it shall be measured to you again. And why beholdest thou the mote that is in thy brother's eye, but considerest not the beam that is in thine own eye?"

I think it would be wise to sweep around our own front doors before we try to sweep around others'. We need to take six months to mind our own business and six months to leave other folks' business alone. In my opinion, they covered up for the man and exposed the woman. We have people who are doing the same thing in this day and time. I once heard a preacher say she was talking to a man about another preacher who God had saved and delivered. The man said, "I don't like that preacher because he committed adultery on his wife." The pastor then asked him who was his favorite Bible hero. The man replied, "King David." The pastor then said, "King David committed adultery with Bathsheba, and he had her husband Uriah killed." The man was left baffled and astonished because he had no knowledge that King David had committed adultery and had Bathsheba's husband Uriah killed. Had this man had the knowledge of King David's history, he wouldn't have spoken so rashly. Hosea 4:6 says, "My people are destroyed for the lack of knowledge." Before we pass judgment on someone else, just remember some of the greatest heroes were not squeaky clean. Some of them had flaws, some made mistakes, and some of them felt inadequate. Noah got drunk. Abraham was too old. Isaac was a daydreamer. Jacob was a liar. Moses was a murderer, and he couldn't talk. Rahab was a prostitute. David was a murderer and adulterer. Elijah was suicidal. Isaiah preached naked. Peter denied Christ. Jonah ran from God. Mary Magdalene was demon possessed. But God! Don't let your past define you; let it redefine you. Your past mistakes and failures can no longer hold you or define you. You made a mistake, but you are not a mistake.

I can recall using white-out in school. If you made a mistake, you could white it out and write over it. This is why I love God because His blood cleansed us from the stain of sin. "Purge me with hyssop, and I shall be clean; wash me, and I shall be whiter than snow" (Psalm 51:7, KJV). God has rewritten your story. Let the redeemed of the Lord say so. If you know it was the Lord who brought you out, you ought to say so. If you know it was the Lord who healed you, restored you, blessed you, saved you, and forgave you, you ought to say so. God has a plan for your life. "For I know the plans I have for you," declares the Lord, "plans to prosper you and not to harm you, plans to give you hope and a future" (Jeremiah 29:11, NIV). God's plans for your life have been predestined before the foundation of the world. His plans are set out for you to succeed and prosper here on earth. God doesn't want to harm you, but help you fulfill your destiny. God knows your beginning and your ending. He is the Alpha and the Omega, the Beginning and the End (Revelation 22:13, NIV).

The right thing to do would have been to bring them both before Jesus if they both were caught committing adultery. These men already knew what the law of Moses said. They were trying to see if Jesus was going to say something that was against the law of Moses. There is no telling how harsh they were with her. I always wondered how they caught them committing adultery? Were they peeping in the window? Were they peeping Toms? It seems to me that they had it in for this woman because in the story, the man is never mentioned. How could she be charged, and they both were caught? How could there be a trial, and the man was not present?

There are many people who have been caught doing wrong, but because of who they were, you never heard about it. People have the tendency to cover up for their friends or people who are in their cliques. Jesus knew that they were trying to trap Him because He knew and understood the law to the letter. After all, they were dealing with the Son of God. Sometimes, people don't know who they are dealing with. I have had many people who already had the answers ask for my input. I had to be very cautious and use discretion in my response because the simple fact is some people are looking for someone to shift the blame onto.

These religious leaders and teachers did not *respect* order because they interrupted the church service just to expose this woman and try to trap Jesus. They did not go to Jesus in private. They exposed this woman publicly. Have you ever had someone try to expose you in front of a crowd? They put her in front of the crowd. "Teacher," they said to Jesus, "this woman was caught in the act of adultery. The law of Moses says to stone her. What do you say?" (John 8:4-5, NLT). They were trying to trap Him into saying something they could use against Him, but Jesus stooped down and wrote in the dust with his finger. I am not sure what Jesus wrote in the dust, but I would probably have written each of the sins they were guilty of. Sometimes, we need to be reminded where we would be or what we would be if it had not been for the Lord on our side. I would have written, "Why are you trying to expose her, and you are guilty yourselves?" This woman could have been stoned to death if it had not been for the love, compassion, and mercy of Jesus. He had to act as though He heard nothing they were saying. We must be quick to listen and slow to speak. It is not always easy to be quiet, but I believe we can learn a lot from this story. There must be times in our lives where we ignore those who are demanding an answer and those who are pestering us, trying to make us say something wrong, so they can turn around and use it against us. Those who came to expose the woman were exposed themselves, from the eldest to the youngest. They all were convicted of their own sins. That is why they walked away one by one.

"They kept demanding an answer, so he stood up again and said, "All right, but let the one who has never sinned throw the first stone!" Then he stooped down again and wrote in the dust. When the accusers heard this, they slipped away one by one, beginning with the oldest, until only Jesus was left in the middle of the crowd with the woman" (John 8:7-9, NLT).

I have always heard that a cheater always accuses you of cheating. A liar always accuses you of lying. A thief always accuses you of stealing. I am not sure what sin they were convicted of, but they were just as guilty as she was. Jesus did not condone her sin, but He did not condemn her either. I can hear Jesus saying, "When the dust settles or when the matter has calmed down, you will still be standing." Things that were foggy will be clearer to you. "Then Jesus stood up again and said to the woman, "Where are your accusers? Didn't even one of them condemn you?" No, Lord," she said. And Jesus said, "Neither do I. Go and sin no more" (John 8:10-11, NLT).

Jesus said to the woman, go away and sin no more! Jesus did not condone her sin, nor did He condemn her. Jesus said, "I have not come to call the righteous, but sinners to repentance" (Luke 5:32, NIV). The religious leaders were so focused on trying to trap Jesus and exposing the woman's sin that they were blinded to their own sins. Jesus came to set the captives free! Go away and sin no more! You don't have to do what you used to do! You do not have to live a lifestyle of sin! You do not have to go from man to man or woman to woman! You don't have to commit adultery anymore. You don't have to fornicate anymore. You don't have to lie, cheat, or steal anymore. You are better than that. God still has a plan for your life! Shake off depression! Shake off those shackles! "Shake off your dust; rise up, sit enthroned, Jerusalem. Free yourself from the chains on your neck, Daughter Zion, now a captive" (Isaiah 52:2, NIV).

When the Apostle Paul was bitten by the viper in Acts 28:3, he shook it off into the fire. Maybe you have been bitten by people who you trusted or by spiritual vipers. After the viper bit Paul, it was still hanging onto his hand. Whatever has been hanging onto you can no longer hold you. According to Acts 28, they thought Paul was a murderer and justice wouldn't let him live, even though he had escaped the sea. How many times have people discerned you wrong, thinking the reason that you were suffering was because you had done something wrong? In their minds, you are reaping what you sowed. Apostle Paul did not wait for anyone to get the viper off of his hand.

He shook it off into the fire and suffered no harm. You cannot wait for anyone else to come to your rescue. They were watching and waiting for him to swell up and die, but after waiting a long time, they changed their minds about him, and said he was a god. There are some people who have seen the attacks against your life, and they thought the attacks were going to take you out. Howbeit, you didn't suffer any harm. You shook them off. Someone is about to change their minds about you. They are going to have to say, "I know that you are a child of God." The same fire that brought it out is the same fire that consumed it. Whatever has been trying to destroy you, shall be destroyed. Shake it off! There's something about getting into an ant bed. Our first instinct is to get out of it and shake ourselves or our clothes. I don't know what or whose ant bed you have been in, but I hear in my spirit, get out of it! Shake yourself loose! Shake yourself free! Shake the ants off.

I hear in my spirit arise, because you have been down too long. If you have been knocked down or sitting down it is time for you to get up. If you have been sleeping on your dreams and visions it is time to wake up, get up, and stay up. Things are shifting for you. Things are turning around for you. God's glory will be seen upon you. "Arise, shine, for your light has come, and the glory of the Lord rises upon you" (Isaiah 60:1, NIV).

It is your time to shine. Most of us can recall the sun shining through our window when it was morning. That was our indication to get up. The light from the sun lit the entire room up. Some of you were probably like me, you didn't care how sleepy you were; you couldn't go back to sleep because the sun was your alarm clock. The sun was your wakeup call. You knew it was time to get up. I don't know who I am talking to, but the sun is shining on you, and you have to get up out of that bed of affliction, sorrow, and betrayal. This book is your alarm clock! You cannot go back to sleep. Wake up and flip the script and tell them don't sleep on me. I'm awake, I'm up, and I'm back! "Loose yourself from the chains around your neck, O captive daughter of Zion" (Isaiah 52:2, NASB).

I have seen and witnessed dogs who were chained up or had collars around their necks. The more the dogs tried to break free, they would find themselves still tied up to the tree. Most people don't fence in dogs or chain up dogs who will not bite. Maybe this is why the enemy has you tied up, attempting to keep you bound, limited, and restricted because he knows that whenever you break free and get loose, your destiny will take off, and your vision is going to take off. Your ministry is going to take off. Your career is going to take off. You are going to get that dream home. You are going to get that business. The devil knows that when you break free, you are going to tear his kingdom down! When a dog gets sick and tired of being sick and tired, no chain, no tree, no owner, or collar can keep it chained. Some of you are sick and tired of living the lifestyle that you are living. Some of you are sick and tired of being in a relationship that is not going anywhere. Some of you are sick and tired of not moving forward. Some of you are sick and tired of being tied down. Now that you are sick and tired of being sick and tired, let me tell you what you need to do. Loose yourself from the chains of your past! It's time to break out and break free, O captive daughter, and be healed from the wounds of your past! I hear the chains falling!

Daily Confessions

These confessions have been created to help you speak your healing, deliverance, and miracles into existence. You can pray the word, speak the word, and decree the word over your life. Life and death are in the power of your tongue. You can have whatsoever you say.

- Confess these "Heal me, O LORD, and I shall be healed; save me, and I shall be saved: for thou art my praise" (Jeremiah 17:14, KJV).
- "He sent his word, and healed them, and delivered them from their destructions" (Psalm 107:20, KJV).
- I am healed from all of my destructions.
- "He heals the broken-hearted and binds up their wounds" (Psalm 147:3, NIV).
- I decree that God is healing your heart and binding up your wounds.
- He is giving me beauty for ashes and the oil of joy for mourning (Isaiah 61:3).

- I've sowed in tears, and now I am about to reap in laughter (Psalm 126:5).
- "Weeping may endure for a night, but joy cometh in the morning" (Psalm 30:5, KJV).
- "As far as the east is from the west, so far hath he removed our transgressions from us" (Psalm 103:12, KJV).
- "I, even I, am he who blots out your transgressions, for my own sake, and remembers your sins no more" (Isaiah 43:25, NIV).
- "Forget the former things; do not dwell on the past. See, I am doing a new thing!" (Isaiah 43:18-19, NIV).
- "Brothers and sisters, I do not consider myself yet to have taken hold of it. But one thing I do: Forgetting what is behind and straining toward what is ahead, I press on toward the goal to win the prize for which God has called me heavenward in Christ Jesus" (Philippians 3:13-14, NIV).

Daily Affirmations

I would like to challenge you to read and confess these affirmations over your life to see a divine change take place. You will be watering your lives with these positive words daily. In order for a plant to grow, it has to be watered—and you are God's plant. I believe that these positive affirmations will prepare you for your healing, deliverance, and miracles.

1. I am healed from the wounds of my past, in Jesus' name!
2. I am an overcomer in Christ Jesus!
3. I am healed from rejection, in Jesus' name!
4. I am healed from mental torment, in Jesus' name!
5. I am healed from bitterness, in Jesus' name!
6. I am healed from unforgiveness, in Jesus' name!
7. I am healed from insecurity, in Jesus' name!

8. I am healed from shame, in Jesus' name!
9. I am healed from anger, in Jesus' name!
10. I am healed from resentment, in Jesus' name!
11. I am healed from hurt, in Jesus' name!
12. I am healed from depression, in Jesus' name!
13. I am healed from oppression, in Jesus' name!
14. I am healed from sickness, in Jesus' name!
15. I am healed from cancer, in Jesus' name!
16. I am healed from diabetes, in Jesus' name!
17. I am healed from heart disease, in Jesus' name
18. I am healed from high blood pressure, in Jesus' name!
19. I am healed from fear, in Jesus' name!
20. I am healed from anxiety attacks, in Jesus' name!
21. I am healed from childhood abuse, in Jesus' name!

22. I am healed from childhood neglect, in Jesus' name!
23. I am healed from suicidal thoughts, in Jesus' name!
24. I am healed from the spirit of torment, in Jesus' name!
25. I am healed from low self-esteem, in Jesus' name!
26. I am healed from verbal abuse, in Jesus' name!
27. I am healed from alcohol and drug abuse, in Jesus' name!
28. I am healed from sexual abuse, in Jesus' name!
29. I am healed from physical abuse, in Jesus' name!
30. I am healed from self-pity, in Jesus' name!
31. I am healed from betrayal, in Jesus' name!
32. I am healed from mind controlling spirits, in Jesus' name!
33. I am healed from all word curses spoken over my life, in Jesus' name!

34. I am healed and delivered from all generational curses, in Jesus' name!
35. I am healed from abandonment, in Jesus' name!
36. I am healed from a broken heart, in Jesus' name!
37. I decree and declare that life and death are in the power of my tongue, and I can have whatsoever I say, in the mighty name of Jesus!
38. I decree and declare miracles, healing, breakthroughs, deliverance, and restoration, in the mighty name of Jesus.
39. I decree and declare that there will be a divine manifestation behind these confessions, in the mighty name of Jesus!
40. I take authority against all backlashes and retaliation behind these confessions. I decree and declare that God's word will not return unto me void. I seal these confessions in the supreme blood of Jesus Christ. Amen!

Sources

Unless otherwise indicated, scripture quotations are from the Holy Bible, King James Version. All rights reserved.

Scriptures marked BSB are taken from The Holy Bible, Berean Study Bible, BSB Copyright ©2016 by Bible Hub. Used by Permission. All Rights Reserved Worldwide.

Scriptures marked NCV are taken from the New Century Version®. Copyright © 2005 by Thomas Nelson. Used by permission. All rights reserved.

Scriptures marked ESV are taken from English Standard Version®. Copyright © 2001 by Crossway, a publishing ministry of Good News Publishers. All rights reserved.

Scriptures marked HCSB are taken from Holman Christian Standard Bible® Copyright © 1999, 2000, 2002, 2003, 2009 by Holman Bible Publishers. Used with permission by Holman Bible Publishers, Nashville, Tennessee. All rights reserved.

Scriptures marked NASB are taken from the New American Standard Bible®. Copyright © 1960, 1962, 1963, 1968, 1971, 1972, 1973, 1975, 1977, 1995 by The Lockman Foundation. Used by permission.

Scriptures marked NCV are taken from the New Century Version®. Copyright © 2005 by Thomas Nelson. Used by permission. All rights reserved.

Scriptures marked NIV are taken from the New International Version®. Copyright © 1973, 1978, 1984, 2011 by Biblica, Inc.™. All rights reserved.

Scriptures marked NKJV are taken from the New King James Version®. Copyright © 1982 by Thomas Nelson. All rights reserved.

Scriptures marked NLT are taken from the New Living Translation®. Copyright © 1996, 2004, 2007, 2013 by Tyndale House Foundation. All rights reserved.

Scriptures marked NLV are taken from the *New Life Version*, copyright © 1969 and 2003. Used by permission of Barbour Publishing, Inc., Uhrichsville, Ohio 44683. All rights reserved.

About the Author

Pastor Addie Kennebrew is a teacher, counselor, mentor, philanthropist, and the founder and senior pastor of the International Worship Center, Inc., in Tallassee, Alabama. She has a bachelor's degree in sociology and is pursuing a master's in human services counseling. One of her most cherished accomplishments is the establishment of the Love, Hope, and Restoration Center, a women's shelter where women are provided short-term living accommodations and are trained, equipped, and empowered to rise above life's challenges.

Pastor Kennebrew firmly believes that God will take your mess and give you a message. She has organized programs to give back to the community by giving away school supplies and clothing, and helping the broken, hurting, and battered. She has provided meals for the less fortunate and those who were incarcerated for the holidays. Her hobbies include reading, swimming, shopping, and traveling. Her life is evidence that it doesn't matter how you start in life but how you end.

To connect, email her at
pastorkennebrew@yahoo.com

CREATING DISTINCTIVE BOOKS
WITH INTENTIONAL RESULTS

We're a collaborative group of creative masterminds with a mission to produce high-quality books to position you for monumental success in the marketplace.

Our professional team of writers, editors, designers, and marketing strategists work closely together to ensure that every detail of your book is a clear representation of the message in your writing.

Want to know more?
Write to us at info@publishyourgift.com
or call (888) 949-6228

Discover great books, exclusive offers, and more at
www.PublishYourGift.com

Connect with us on social media

@publishyourgift

www.ingramcontent.com/pod-product-compliance
Lightning Source LLC
Chambersburg PA
CBHW070949080526
44587CB00015B/2246